The
Village
and other poems

Oliver Goldsmith

A Phoenix Paperback

This edition first published in 1996 by Phoenix
a division of Orion Books Ltd
Orion House, 5 Upper St Martin's Lane, London WC2H 9EA

Cover illustration: 'Storm on the Heath' by English School (19th Century),
Agnew & Sons, London (Bridgeman Art Library, London)

ISBN 1 85799 661 5

Typeset by Deltatype Ltd, Ellesmere Port, Cheshire
Printed and bound in Great Britain
by Clays Ltd, St Ives plc

CONTENTS

The Deserted Village

Sweet Auburn! loveliest village of the plain,
Where health and plenty cheer'd the labouring swain,
Where smiling spring its earliest visit paid,
And parting summer's lingering blooms delay'd:
Dear lovely bowers of innocence and ease,
Seats of my youth, when every sport could please,
How often have I loiter'd o'er thy green,
Where humble happiness endear'd each scene;
How often have I paus'd on every charm,
The shelter'd cot, the cultivated farm,
The never-failing brook, the busy mill,
The decent church that topp'd the neighbouring hill,
The hawthorn bush, with seats beneath the shade,
For talking age and whisp'ring lovers made;
How often have I bless'd the coming day,
When toil remitting lent its turn to play,
And all the village train, from labour free,
Led up their sports beneath the spreading tree;
While many a pastime circled in the shade,
The young contending as the old survey'd;
And many a gambol frolick'd o'er the ground,
And sleights of art and feats of strength went round;
And still as each repeated pleasure tir'd,

Succeeding sports the mirthful band inspir'd;
The dancing pair that simply sought renown,
By holding out to tire each other down;
The swain mistrustless of his smutted face,
While secret laughter titter'd round the place;
The bashful virgin's side-long looks of love,
The matron's glance that would those looks reprove;
These were thy charms, sweet village; sports like these,
With sweet succession, taught e'en toil to please;
These round thy bowers their cheerful influence shed,
These were thy charms – But all these charms are fled.

Sweet smiling village, loveliest of the lawn,
Thy sports are fled, and all thy charms withdrawn;
Amidst thy bowers the tyrant's hand is seen,
And desolation saddens all thy green:
One only master grasps the whole domain,
And half a tillage stints thy smiling plain:
No more thy glassy brook reflects the day,
But chok'd with sedges, works its weedy way.
Along thy glades, a solitary guest,
The hollow-sounding bittern guards its nest;
Amidst thy desert walks the lapwing flies,
And tires their echoes with unvaried cries.
Sunk are thy bowers in shapeless ruin all,
And the long grass o'ertops the mould'ring wall;
And trembling, shrinking from the spoiler's hand,
Far, far away, thy children leave the land.

Ill fares the land, to hast'ning ills a prey,
Where wealth accumulates, and men decay:
Princes and lords may flourish, or may fade;
A breath can make them, as a breath has made;
But a bold peasantry, their country's pride,
When once destroy'd, can never be supplied.

A time there was, ere England's griefs began,
When every rood of ground maintain'd its man;
For him light labour spread her wholesome store,
Just gave what life requir'd, but gave no more:
His best companions, innocence and health;
And his best riches, ignorance of wealth.

But times are alter'd; trade's unfeeling train
Usurp the land and dispossess the swain;
Along the lawn, where scatter'd hamlets rose,
Unwieldy wealth, and cumbrous pomp repose;
And every want to opulence allied,
And every pang that folly pays to pride.
Those gentle hours that plenty bade to bloom,
Those calm desires that ask'd but little room,
Those healthful sports that grac'd the peaceful scene,
Liv'd in each look, and brighten'd all the green;
These, far departing, seek a kinder shore,
And rural mirth and manners are no more.

Sweet Auburn! parent of the blissful hour,
Thy glades forlorn confess the tyrant's power.

Here as I take my solitary rounds,
Amidst thy tangling walks, and ruin'd grounds,
And, many a year elaps'd, return to view
Where once the cottage stood, the hawthorn grew,
Remembrance wakes with all her busy train,
Swells at my breast, and turns the past to pain.

In all my wand'rings round this world of care,
In all my griefs – and God has given my share –
I still had hopes my latest hours to crown,
Amidst these humble bowers to lay me down;
To husband out life's taper at the close,
And keep the flame from wasting by repose.
I still had hopes, for pride attends us still,
Amidst the swains to show my book-learn'd skill,
Around my fire an evening group to draw,
And tell of all I felt, and all I saw;
And, as a hare, whom hounds and horns pursue,
Pants to the place from whence at first she flew,
I still had hopes, my long vexations pass'd,
Here to return – and die at home at last.

O blest retirement, friend to life's decline,
Retreats from care, that never must be mine,
How happy he who crowns in shades like these,
A youth of labour with an age of ease;
Who quits a world where strong temptations try
And, since 'tis hard to combat, learns to fly!

For him no wretches, born to work and weep,
Explore the mine, or tempt the dangerous deep;
No surly porter stands in guilty state
To spurn imploring famine from the gate;
But on he moves to meet his latter end,
Angels around befriending Virtue's friend;
Bends to the grave with unperceiv'd decay,
While Resignation gently slopes the way;
And, all his prospects bright'ning to the last,
His Heaven commences ere the world be pass'd!

Sweet was the sound, when oft at evening's close
Up yonder hill the village murmur rose;
There, as I pass'd with careless steps and slow,
The mingling notes came soften'd from below;
The swain responsive as the milk-maid sung,
The sober herd that low'd to meet their young;
The noisy geese that gabbled o'er the pool,
The playful children just let loose from school;
The watchdog's voice that bay'd the whisp'ring wind,
And the loud laugh that spoke the vacant mind;
These all in sweet confusion sought the shade,
And fill'd each pause the nightingale had made.
But now the sounds of population fail,
No cheerful murmurs fluctuate in the gale,
No busy steps the grass-grown foot-way tread,
For all the bloomy flush of life is fled.
All but yon widow'd, solitary thing

That feebly bends beside the plashy spring;
She, wretched matron, forc'd, in age, for bread,
To strip the brook with mantling cresses spread,
To pick her wintry faggot from the thorn,
To seek her nightly shed, and weep till morn;
She only left of all the harmless train,
The sad historian of the pensive plain.

Near yonder copse, where once the garden smil'd,
And still where many a garden flower grows wild;
There, where a few torn shrubs the place disclose,
The village preacher's modest mansion rose.
A man he was to all the country dear,
And passing rich with forty pounds a year;
Remote from towns he ran his godly race,
Nor e'er had chang'd, nor wished to change his place;
Unpractis'd he to fawn, or seek for power,
By doctrines fashion'd to the varying hour;
Far other aims his heart had learned to prize,
More skill'd to raise the wretched than to rise.
His house was known to all the vagrant train,
He chid their wand'rings, but reliev'd their pain;
The long-remember'd beggar was his guest,
Whose beard descending swept his aged breast;
The ruin'd spendthrift, now no longer proud,
Claim'd kindred there, and had his claims allow'd;
The broken soldier, kindly bade to stay,
Sat by his fire, and talk'd the night away;

Wept o'er his wounds, or tales of sorrow done,
Shoulder'd his crutch, and show'd how fields were won.
Pleas'd with his guests, the good man learn'd to glow,
And quite forgot their vices in their woe;
Careless their merits, or their faults to scan,
His pity gave ere charity began

Thus to relieve the wretched was his pride,
And e'en his failings lean'd to Virtue's side;
But in his duty prompt at every call,
He watch'd and wept, he pray'd and felt, for all.
And, as a bird each fond endearment tries
To tempt its new-fledg'd offspring to the skies,
He tried each art, reprov'd each dull delay,
Allur'd to brighter worlds, and led the way.

Beside the bed where parting life was laid,
And sorrow, guilt, and pain, by turns dismay'd,
The reverend champion stood. At his control,
Despair and anguish fled the struggling soul;
Comfort came down the trembling wretch to raise,
And his last falt'ring accents whisper'd praise.
At church, with meek and unaffected grace,
His looks adorn'd the venerable place;
Truth from his lips prevail'd with double sway,
And fools, who came to scoff, remain'd to pray.
The service pass'd, around the pious man,
With steady zeal, each honest rustic ran;

Even children follow'd with endearing wile,
And pluck'd his gown, to share the good man's smile.
His ready smile a parent's warmth express'd,
Their welfare pleas'd him, and their cares distress'd;
To them his heart, his love, his griefs were given,
But all his serious thoughts had rest in Heaven.
As some tall cliff, that lifts its awful form,
Swells from the vale, and midway leaves the storm,
Though round its breast the rolling clouds are spread,
Eternal sunshine settles on its head.

Beside yon straggling fence that skirts the way,
With blossom'd furze unprofitably gay,
There, in his noisy mansion, skill'd to rule,
The village master taught his little school;
A man severe he was, and stern to view;
I knew him well, and every truant knew;
Well had the boding tremblers learn'd to trace
The day's disasters in his morning face;
Full well they laugh'd, with counterfeited glee,
At all his jokes, for many a joke had he;
Full well the busy whisper, circling round,
Convey'd the dismal tidings when he frown'd;
Yet he was kind; or if severe in aught,
The love he bore to learning was in fault;
The village all declar'd how much he knew;
'Twas certain he could write, and cypher too;
Lands he could measure, terms and tides presage,

And e'en the story ran that he could gauge.
In arguing too, the parson own'd his skill,
For e'en though vanquish'd, he could argue still;
While words of learned length and thund'ring sound
Amazed the gazing rustics rang'd around,
And still they gaz'd, and still the wonder grew,
That one small head could carry all he knew.

But past is all his fame. The very spot
Where many a time he triumph'd, is forgot.
Near yonder thorn, that lifts its head on high,
Where once the sign-post caught the passing eye,
Low lies that house where nut-brown draughts inspir'd,
Where grey-beard mirth and smiling toil retir'd,
Where village statesman talk'd with looks profound,
And news much older than their ale went round.
Imagination fondly stoops to trace
The parlour splendours of that festive place;
The white-wash'd wall, the nicely sanded floor,
The varnish'd clock that click'd behind the door;
The chest contriv'd a double debt to pay,
A bed by night, a chest of drawers by day;
The pictures plac'd for ornament and use,
The twelve good rules, the royal game of goose;
The hearth, except when winter chill'd the day,
With aspen boughs, and flowers, and fennel gay;
While broken tea-cups, wisely kept for show,
Rang'd o'er the chimney, glisten'd in a row.

Vain, transitory splendours! Could not all
Reprieve the tottering mansion from its fall!
Obscure it sinks, nor shall it more impart
An hour's importance to the poor man's heart;
Thither no more the peasant shall repair
To sweet oblivion of his daily care;
No more the farmer's news, the barber's tale,
No more the wood-man's ballad shall prevail;
No more the smith his dusky brow shall clear,
Relax his pond'rous strength, and lean to hear;
The host himself no longer shall be found
Careful to see the mantling bliss go round;
Nor the coy maid, half willing to be press'd,
Shall kiss the cup to pass it to the rest.

Yes! let the rich deride, the proud disdain,
These simple blessings of the lowly train;
To me more dear, congenial to my heart,
One native charm, than all the gloss of art;
Spontaneous joys, where Nature has its play,
The soul adopts, and owns their first-born sway;
Lightly they frolic o'er the vacant mind,
Unenvied, unmolested, unconfin'd:
But the long pomp, the midnight masquerade,
With all the freaks of wanton wealth array'd,
In these, ere triflers half their wish obtain,
The toiling pleasure sickens into pain;
And, e'en while fashion's brightest arts decoy,
The heart distrusting asks, if this be joy.

Ye friends to truth, ye statesmen, who survey
The rich man's joys increase, the poor's decay,
'Tis yours to judge, how wide the limits stand
Between a splendid and a happy land.
Proud swells the tide with loads of freighted ore,
And shouting Folly hails them from her shore;
Hoards, e'en beyond the miser's wish abound,
And rich men flock from all the world around.
Yet count our gains. This wealth is but a name
That leaves our useful products still the same.
Not so the loss. The man of wealth and pride
Takes up a space that many poor supplied;
Space for his lake, his park's extended bounds,
Space for his horses, equipage, and hounds;
The robe that wraps his limbs in silken sloth
Has robb'd the neighbouring fields of half their growth,
His seat, where solitary sports are seen,
Indignant spurns the cottage from the green;
Around the world each needful product flies,
For all the luxuries the world supplies:
While thus the land adorn'd for pleasure, all
In barren splendour feebly waits the fall.

As some fair female unadorn'd and plain,
Secure to please while youth confirms her reign,
Slights every borrow'd charm that dress supplies,
Nor shares with art the triumph of her eyes:
But when those charms are pass'd, for charms are frail.

When time advances, and when lovers fail,
She then shines forth, solicitous to bless,
In all the glaring impotence of dress.
Thus fares the land, by luxury betray'd,
In nature's simplest charms at first array'd;
But verging to decline, its splendours rise,
Its vistas strike, its palaces surprise;
While scourg'd by famine from the smiling land,
The mournful peasant leads his humble band;
And while he sinks, without one arm to save,
The country blooms – a garden, and a grave.

Where then, ah! where, shall poverty reside,
To 'scape the pressure of contiguous pride?
If to some common's fenceless limits stray'd,
He drives his flock to pick the scanty blade,
Those fenceless fields the sons of wealth divide,
And e'en the bare-worn common is denied.

If to the city sped – What waits him there?
To see profusion that he must not share;
To see ten thousand baneful arts combin'd
To pamper luxury and thin mankind;
To see those joys the sons of pleasure know
Extorted from his fellow creature's woe.
Here, while the courtier glitters in brocade,
There the pale artist plies the sickly trade;
Here, while the proud their long-drawn pomps display,

There the black gibbet glooms beside the way.
The dome where Pleasure holds her midnight reign
Here, richly deck'd, admits the gorgeous train;
Tumultuous grandeur crowds the blazing square,
The rattling chariots clash, the torches glare.
Sure scenes like these no troubles e'er annoy!
Sure these denote one universal joy!
Are these thy serious thoughts? – Ah, turn thine eyes
Where the poor houseless shiv'ring female lies.
She once, perhaps, in village plenty bless'd,
Has wept at tales of innocence distress'd;
Her modest looks the cottage might adorn,
Sweet as the primrose peeps beneath the thorn;
Now lost to all; her friends, her virtue fled,
Near her betrayer's door she lays her head,
And, pinch'd with cold, and shrinking from the shower,
With heavy heart deplores that luckless hour,
When idly first, ambitious of the town,
She left her wheel and robes of country brown.

Do thine, sweet Auburn, thine, the loveliest train
Do thy fair tribes participate her pain?
E'en now, perhaps, by cold and hunger led,
At proud men's doors they ask a little bread!

Ah, no. To distant climes, a dreary scene,
Where half the convex world intrudes between,
Through torrid tracts with fainting steps they go,

13

Where wild Altama murmurs to their woe.
Far different there from all that charm'd before,
The various terrors of that horrid shore;
Those blazing suns that dart a downward ray,
And fiercely shed intolerable day;
Those matted woods where birds forget to sing,
But silent bats in drowsy clusters cling;
Those pois'nous fields with rank luxuriance crown'd,
Where the dark scorpion gathers death around;
Where at each step the stranger fears to wake
The rattling terrors of the vengeful snake;
Where crouching tigers wait their hapless prey
And savage men more murd'rous still than they;
While oft in whirls the mad tornado flies,
Mingling the ravag'd landscape with the skies.
Far different these from every former scene,
The cooling brook, the grassy-vested green,
The breezy covert of the warbling grove,
That only shelter'd thefts of harmless love.

Good heaven! what sorrows gloom'd that parting day,
That call'd them from their native walks away;
When the poor exiles, every pleasure pass'd,
Hung round their bowers, and fondly look'd their last,
And took a long farewell, and wish'd in vain
For seats like these beyond the western main;
And shudd'ring still to face the distant deep,
Return'd and wept, and still return'd to weep.

The good old sire, the first prepar'd to go
To new-found worlds, and wept for others' woe;
But for himself, in conscious virtue brave,
He only wish'd for worlds beyond the grave.
His lovely daughter, lovelier in her tears,
The fond companion of his helpless years,
Silent went next, neglectful of her charms,
And left a lover's for a father's arms.
With louder plaints the mother spoke her woes,
And bless'd the cot where every pleasure rose
And kiss'd her thoughtless babes with many a tear,
And clasp'd them close, in sorrow doubly dear;
Whilst her fond husband strove to lend relief
In all the silent manliness of grief.

O Luxury! thou curs'd by Heaven's decree,
How ill exchang'd are things like these for thee!
How do thy potions, with insidious joy
Diffuse their pleasure only to destroy!
Kingdoms, by thee, to sickly greatness grown,
Boast of a florid vigour not their own;
At every draught more large and large they grow,
A bloated mass of rank unwieldy woe;
Till sapp'd their strength, and every part unsound,
Down, down they sink, and spread a ruin round.

E'en now the devastation is begun,
And half the business of destruction done;

E'en now, methinks, as pond'ring here I stand,
I see the rural virtues leave the land:
Down where yon anchoring vessel spreads the sail,
That idly waiting flaps with ev'ry gale,
Downward they move, a melancholy band,
Pass from the shore, and darken all the strand.
Contented toil, and hospitable care,
And kind connubial tenderness, are there;
And piety, with wishes plac'd above,
And steady loyalty, and faithful love.
And thou, sweet Poetry, thou loveliest maid,
Still first to fly where sensual joys invade;
Unfit in these degenerate times of shame,
To catch the heart, or strike for honest fame;
Dear charming nymph, neglected and decried,
My shame in crowds, my solitary pride;
Thou source of all my bliss, and all my woe,
That found'st me poor at first, and keep'st me so;
Thou guide by which the nobler arts excel,
Thou nurse of every virtue, fare thee well!
Farewell, and Oh! where'er thy voice be tried,
On Torno's cliffs, or Pambamarca's side,
Whether where equinoctial fervours glow,
Or winter wraps the polar world in snow,
Still let thy voice, prevailing over time,
Redress the rigours of th' inclement clime;
Aid slighted truth; with thy persuasive strain
Teach erring man to spurn the rage of gain;

Teach him, that states of native strength possess'd,
Though very poor, may still be very bless'd;
That trade's proud empire hastes to swift decay,
As ocean sweeps the labour'd mole away;
While self-dependent power can time defy,
As rocks resist the billows and the sky.

On a Beautiful Youth Struck Blind with Lightning

(*Imitated from the Spanish.*)

Sure 'twas by Providence design'd,
    Rather in pity, than in hate,
That he should be, like Cupid, blind,
    To save him from Narcissus' fate.

The Gift

TO IRIS, IN BOW STREET, COVENT GARDEN

Say, cruel Iris, pretty rake,
    Dear mercenary beauty,
What annual offering shall I make,
    Expressive of my duty?

My heart, a victim to thine eyes,
    Should I at once deliver,

17

Say, would the angry fair one prize
    The gift, who slights the giver?

A bill, a jewel, watch, or toy,
    My rivals give – and let 'em;
If gems, or gold, impart a joy,
    I'll give them – when I get 'em.

I'll give – but not the full-blown rose,
    Or rose-bud more in fashion;
Such short-liv'd offerings but disclose
    A transitory passion.

I'll give thee something yet unpaid,
    Not less sincere, than civil;
I'll give thee – Ah! too charming maid,
    I'll give thee – To the devil.

The Logicians Refuted

IN IMITATION OF DEAN SWIFT

Logicians have but ill defin'd
As rational, the human kind;
Reason, they say, belongs to man,
But let them prove it if they can.

Wise Aristotle and Smiglecius,
By ratiocinations specious,
Have strove to prove with great precision,
With definition and division,
Homo est ratione praeditum, –
But for my soul I cannot credit 'em;
And must in spite of them maintain,
That man and all his ways are vain;
And that this boasted lord of nature
Is both a weak and erring creature;
That instinct is a surer guide
Than reason-boasting mortals' pride;
And that brute beasts are far before 'em,
Deus est anima brutorum.
Who ever knew an honest brute
At law his neighbour prosecute,
Bring action for assault and battery,
Or friend beguile with lies and flattery?
O'er plains they ramble unconfin'd,
No politics disturb their mind;
They eat their meals, and take their sport,
Nor know who's in or out at court;
They never to the levee go
To treat as dearest friend, a foe;
They never importune his grace,
Nor ever cringe to men in place;
Nor undertake a dirty job,
Nor draw the quill to write for B–b.

Fraught with invective they ne'er go
To folks at Pater-Noster-Row;
No judges, fiddlers, dancing-masters,
No pick-pockets, or poetasters,
Are known to honest quadrupeds;
No single brute his fellow leads.
Brutes never meet in bloody fray,
Nor cut each others' throats, for pay
Of beasts, it is confess'd, the ape
Comes nearest us in human shape;
Like man he imitates each fashion.
And malice is his ruling passion;
But both in malice and grimaces
A courtier any ape surpasses.
Behold him humbly cringing wait
Upon a minister of state;
View him soon after to inferiors,
Aping the conduct of superiors;
He promises with equal air,
And to perform takes equal care.
He in his turn finds imitators;
At court, the porters, lacqueys, waiters,
Their master's manners still contract,
And footmen, lords and dukes can act.
Thus at the court both great and small
Behave alike – for all ape all.

A Sonnet

Weeping, murmuring, complaining,
    Lost to every gay delight;
Myra, too sincere for feigning,
    Fears th' approaching bridal night.

Yet, why impair thy bright perfection?
    Or dim thy beauty with a tear?
Had Myra followed my direction,
    She long had wanted cause of fear.

An Elegy On That Glory Of Her Sex, Mrs Mary Blaize

Good people all, with one accord,
    Lament for Madam Blaize,
Who never wanted a good word –
    From those who spoke her praise.

The needy seldom pass'd her door,
    And always found her kind;
She freely lent to all the poor, –
    Who left a pledge behind.

She strove the neighbourhood to please,
    With manners wond'rous winning,

And never follow'd wicked ways, –
　　Unless when she was sinning.

At church, in silks and satins new,
　　With hoop of wondrous size,
She never slumber'd in her pew, –
　　But when she shut her eyes.

Her love was sought, I do aver,
　　By twenty beaux and more;
The king himself has follow'd her, –
　　When she has walk'd before.

But now her wealth and finery fled,
　　Her hangers-on cut short all;
The doctors found, when she was dead, –
　　Her last disorder mortal.

Let us lament, in sorrow sore,
　　For Kent-street well may say,
That had she liv'd a twelve-month more, –
　　She had not died today.

Description Of An Author's Bedchamber

Where the Red Lion flaring o'er the way,
Invites each passing stranger that can pay;

Where Calvert's butt, and Parson's black champagne,
Regale the drabs and bloods of Drury-lane;
There in a lonely room, from bailiffs snug,
The Muse found Scroggen stretch'd beneath a rug;
A window, patch'd with paper, lent a ray,
That dimly show'd the state in which he lay;
The sanded floor that grits beneath the tread;
The humid wall with paltry pictures spread:
The royal game of goose was there in view,
And the twelve rules the royal martyr drew;
The seasons, fram'd with listing, found a place,
And brave prince William show'd his lamp-black face:
The morn was cold, he views with keen desire
The rusty grate unconscious of a fire;
With beer and milk arrears the frieze was scor'd,
And five crack'd teacups dress'd the chimney board;
A nightcap deck'd his brows instead of bay,
A cap by night – a stocking all the day!

Translation Of A South American Ode

In all my Enna's beauties blest,
    Amidst profusion still I pine;
For though she gives me up her breast,
    Its panting tenant is not mine.

The Double Transformation

Secluded from domestic strife,
Jack Book-worm led a college life;
A fellowship at twenty-five
Made him the happiest man alive;
He drank his glass and crack'd his joke,
And freshmen wonder'd as he spoke.

Such pleasures, unalloy'd with care,
Could any accident impair?
Could Cupid's shaft at length transfix
Our Swain, arriv'd at thirty-six?
O had the archer ne'er come down
To ravage in a country town!
Or Flavia been content to stop
At triumphs in a Fleet-street shop.
O had her eyes forgot to blaze!
Or Jack had wanted eyes to gaze.
O! – But let exclamation cease,
Her presence banish'd all his peace.
So with decorum all things carried;
Miss frown'd, and blush'd, and then was – married.

Need we expose to vulgar sight
The raptures of the bridal night?

Need we intrude on hallow'd ground,
Or draw the curtains clos'd around?
Let it suffice, that each had charms;
He clasp'd a goddess in his arms;
And, though she felt his usage rough,
Yet in a man 'twas well enough.

The honey-moon like lightning flew,
The second brought its transport too.
A third, a fourth, were not amiss,
The fifth was friendship mix'd with bliss:
But, when a twelvemonth pass'd away,
Jack found his goddess made of clay;
Found half the charms that deck'd her face
Arose from powder, shreds, or lace;
But still the worst remain'd behind,
That very face had robb'd her mind.

Skill'd in no other arts was she,
But dressing, patching, repartee;
And, just as humour rose or fell,
By turns a slattern or a belle:
'Tis true she dress'd with modern grace,
Half naked at a ball or race;
But when at home, at board or bed,
Five greasy nightcaps wrapp'd her head.
Could so much beauty condescend
To be a dull domestic friend?

Could any curtain-lectures bring
To decency so fine a thing?
In short, by night, 'twas fits or fretting;
By day, 'twas gadding or coquetting.
Fond to be seen, she kept a bevy
Of powder'd coxcombs at her levy;
The 'squire and captain took their stations,
And twenty other near relations;
Jack suck'd his pipe, and often broke
A sigh in suffocating smoke;
While all their hours were pass'd between
Insulting repartee or spleen.

Thus as her faults each day were known,
He thinks her features coarser grown;
He fancies every vice she shows,
Or thins her lip, or points her nose:
Whenever rage or envy rise,
How wide her mouth, how wild her eyes!
He knows not how, but so it is,
Her face is grown a knowing phiz;
And, though her fops are wond'rous civil,
He thinks her ugly as the devil.

Now, to perplex the ravell'd noose,
As each a different way pursues,
While sullen or loquacious strife,
Promis'd to hold them on for life,

That dire disease, whose ruthless power
Withers the beauty's transient flower:
Lo! the small-pox, whose horrid glare
Levell'd its terrors at the fair;
And, rifling ev'ry youthful grace,
Left but the remnant of a face.

The glass, grown hateful to her sight,
Reflected now a perfect fright:
Each former art she vainly tries
To bring back lustre to her eyes.
In vain she tries her paste and creams,
To smooth her skin, or hide its seams;
Her country beaux and city cousins,
Lovers no more, flew off by dozens:
The 'squire himself was seen to yield,
And e'en the captain quit the field.

Poor Madam, now condemn'd to hack
The rest of life with anxious Jack,
Perceiving others fairly flown,
Attempted pleasing him alone.
Jack soon was dazzl'd to behold
Her present face surpass the old;
With modesty her cheeks are dy'd,
Humility displaces pride;
For tawdry finery is seen
A person ever neatly clean:

No more presuming on her sway,
She learns good-nature every day;
Serenely gay, and strict in duty,
Jack finds his wife a perfect beauty.

Edwin And Angelina

A BALLAD

'Turn, gentle hermit of the dale,
    And guide my lonely way,
To where yon taper cheers the vale
    With hospitable ray.

'For here, forlorn and lost I tread,
    With fainting steps and slow;
Where wilds immeasurably spread,
    Seem length'ning as I go.'

'Forbear, my son,' the hermit cries,
    'To tempt the dangerous gloom;
For yonder faithless phantom flies
    To lure thee to thy doom.

'Here to the houseless child of want
    My door is open still;
And though my portion is but scant,
    I give it with good will.

'Then turn to-night, and freely share
  Whate'er my cell bestows;
My rushy couch, and frugal fare,
  My blessing and repose.

'No flocks that range the valley free
  To slaughter I condemn:
Taught by that power that pities me,
  I learn to pity them.

'But from the mountain's grassy side
  A guiltless feast I bring;
A scrip with herbs and fruits supplied,
  And water from the spring.

'Then, pilgrim, turn, thy cares forego;
  All earth-born cares are wrong:
Man wants but little here below,
  Nor wants that little long.'

Soft as the dew from heav'n descends,
  His gentle accents fell:
The modest stranger lowly bends,
  And follows to the cell.

Far in a wilderness obscure
  The lonely mansion lay;
A refuge to the neighbouring poor
  And strangers led astray.

No stores beneath its humble thatch
   Requir'd a master's care;
The wicket, opening with a latch,
   Receiv'd the harmless pair.

And now, when busy crowds retire
   To take their evening rest,
The hermit trimm'd his little fire,
   And cheer'd his pensive guest:

And spread his vegetable store,
   And gaily press'd, and smil'd;
And, skill'd in legendary lore,
   The lingering hours beguil'd.

Around in sympathetic mirth
   Its tricks the kitten tries;
The cricket chirrups in the hearth;
   The crackling faggot flies.

But nothing could a charm impart
   To soothe the stranger's woe;
For grief was heavy at his heart,
   And tears began to flow.

His rising cares the hermit spied,
   With answ'ring care oppress'd;
'And whence, unhappy youth,' he cried,
   'The sorrows of thy breast?

'From better habitations spurn'd,
    Reluctant dost thou rove;
Or grieve for friendship unreturn'd,
    Or unregarded love?

'Alas! the joys that fortune brings
    Are trifling, and decay;
And those who prize the paltry things,
    More trifling still than they

'And what is friendship but a name,
    A charm that lulls to sleep;
A shade that follows wealth or fame,
    But leaves the wretch to weep?

'And love is still an emptier sound,
    The modern fair one's jest:
On earth unseen, or only found
    To warm the turtle's nest.

'For shame, fond youth, thy sorrows hush,
    And spurn the sex,' he said:
But, while he spoke, a rising blush
    His love-lorn guest betray'd.

Surprise'd, he sees new beauties rise,
    Swift mantling to the view;
Like colours o'er the morning skies,
    As bright, as transient too.

The bashful look, the rising breast,
　　Alternate spread alarms:
The lovely stranger stands confess'd
　　A maid in all her charms

'And, ah! forgive a stranger rude,
　　A wretch forlorn,' she cried;
'Whose feet unhallow'd thus intrude
　　Where heaven and you reside.

'But let a maid thy pity share,
　　Whom love has taught to stray;
Who seeks for rest, but finds despair
　　Companion of her way.

'My father liv'd beside the Tyne,
　　A wealthy lord was he;
And all his wealth was mark'd as mine,
　　He had but only me.

'To win me from his tender arms
　　Unnumber'd suitors came;
Who prais'd me for imputed charms,
　　And felt or feign'd a flame.

Each hour a mercenary crowd
　　With richest proffers strove:
Amongst the rest young Edwin bow'd,
　　But never talk'd of love.

'In humble, simplest habit clad,
    No wealth nor power had he;
Wisdom and worth were all he had,
    But these were all to me.

'And when beside me in the dale
    He caroll'd lays of love;
His breath lent fragrance to the gale,
    And music to the grove.

'The blossom opening to the day,
    The dews of heaven refin'd
Could nought of purity display,
    To emulate his mind.

'The dew, the blossom on the tree,
    With charms inconstant shine;
Their charms were his, but woe to me!
    Their constancy was mine.

'For still I tried each fickle art,
    Importunate and vain:
And while his passion touch'd my heart,
    I triumph'd in his pain.

'Till quite dejected with my scorn,
    He left me to my pride;
And sought a solitude forlorn.
    In secret, where he died.   33

'But mine the sorrow, mine the fault,
    And well my life shall pay;
I'll seek the solitude he sought,
    And stretch me where he lay

'And there forlorn, despairing, hid,
    I'll lay me down and die;
'Twas so for me that Edwin did,
    And so for him will I.'

'Forbid it, heaven!' the hermit cried
    And clasp'd her to his breast:
The wondering fair one turn'd to chide,
    'Twas Edwin's self that prest.

'Turn, Angelina, ever dear,
    My charmer, turn to see
Thy own, thy long-lost Edwin here,
    Restor'd to love and thee.

'Thus let me hold thee to my heart,
    And ev'ry care resign;
And shall we never, never part,
    My life – my all that's mine?

'No, never from this hour to part,
    We'll live and love so true;
The sigh that rends thy constant heart
    Shall break thy Edwin's too.'

Elegy on the Death of a Mad Dog

Good people all, of every sort,
    Give ear unto my song;
And if you find it wond'rous short,
    It cannot hold you long.

In Islington there was a man,
    Of whom the world might say,
That still a godly race he ran,
    Whene'er he went to pray.

A kind and gentle heart he had,
    To comfort friends and foes;
The naked every day he clad,
    When he put on his clothes.

And in that town a dog was found,
    As many dogs there be,
Both mongrel, puppy, whelp, and hound,
    And curs of low degree.

This dog and man at first were friends;
    But when a pique began,
The dog, to gain some private ends,
    Went mad and bit the man.

Around from all the neighbouring streets
    The wond'ring neighbours ran,
And swore the dog had lost his wits,
    To bite so good a man.

The wound it seem'd both sore and sad
    To every Christian eye;
And while they swore the dog was mad,
    They swore the man would die.

But soon a wonder came to light,
    That show'd the rogues they lied:
The man recover'd of the bite,
    The dog it was that died.

Song

FROM 'THE VICAR OF WAKEFIELD'

When lovely woman stoops to folly,
    And finds too late that men betray,
What charms can soothe her melancholy,
    What art can wash her guilt away?

The only art her guilt to cover,
    To hide her shame from every eye,
To give repentance to her lover,
    And wring his bosom, is – to die.

A New Simile

(*In the Manner of Swift.*)

Long had I sought in vain to find
A likeness for the scribbling kind;
The modern scribbling kind, who write,
In wit, and sense, and nature's spite:
'Till reading, I forget what day on,
A chapter out of Took's Pantheon;
I think I met with something there,
To suit my purpose to a hair;
But let us not proceed too furious,
First please to turn to God Mercurius;
You'll find him pictured at full length
In book the second, page the tenth:
The stress of all my proofs on him I lay,
And now proceed we to our simile

Imprimis, pray observe his hat
Wings upon either side – mark that.
Well! what is it from thence we gather?
Why these denote a brain of feather.
A brain of feather! very right,
With wit that's flighty, learning light;
Such as to modern bard's decreed:
A just comparison, – proceed.

In the next place, his feet peruse,
Wings grow again from both his shoes;
Design'd no doubt, their part to bear,
And waft his godship through the air;
And here my simile unites,
For in a modern poet's flights,
I'm sure it may be justly said,
His feet are useful as his head.

Lastly, vouchsafe t' observe his hand,
Fill'd with a snake incircled wand;
By classic authors, term'd caducis,
And highly fam'd for several uses.
To wit – most wond'rously endu'd,
No poppy water half so good;
For let folks only get a touch,
It's soporific virtue's such,
Tho' ne'er so much awake before,
That quickly they begin to snore.
Add too, what certain writers tell,
With this he drives men's souls to hell.

Now to apply, begin we then;
His wand's a modern author's pen;
The serpents round about it twin'd,
Denote him of the reptile kind;
Denote the rage with which he writes,
His frothy slaver, venom'd bites;

An equal semblance still to keep,
Alike too, both conduce to sleep.
This diff'rence only, as the God,
Drove soul's to Tart'rus with his rod;
With his goosequill the scribbling elf,
Instead of others, damns himself.

And here my simile almost tript,
Yet grant a word by way of postscript,
Moreover, Merc'ry had a failing:
Well! what of that? out with it – stealing;
In which all modern bards agree,
Being each as great a thief as he:
But ev'n this deities' existence,
Shall lend my simile assistance.
Our modern bards! why what a pox
Are they but senseless stones and blocks?

Verses in Reply to an Invitation to Dinner at Dr Baker's

Your mandate I got,
You may all go to pot;
Had your senses been right,
You'd have sent before night;
As I hope to be saved,
I put off being shaved;

For I could not make bold,
While the matter was cold,
To meddle in suds,
Or to put on my duds;
So tell Horneck and Nesbitt,
And Baker and his bit,
And Kauffman beside,
And the Jessamy bridge,
With the rest of the crew,
The Reynoldses two,
Little Comedy's face,
And the Captain in lace.
(By the bye you may tell him,
I have something to sell him;
Of use I insist,
When he comes to enlist.
Your worships must know
That a few days ago,
An order went out,
For the foot guards so stout
To wear tails in high taste,
Twelve inches at least:
Now I've got him a scale
To measure each tail,
And a long one to curtail.) –
   Yet how can I when vext,
Thus stray from my text?
Tell each other to rue

Your Devonshire crew,
For sending so late
To one of my state.
But 'tis Reynolds's way
From wisdom to stray,
And Angelica's whim
To be frolick like him,
But, alas! your good worships, how could they be wiser,
When both have been spoil'd in to-day's Advertiser?

OLIVER GOLDSMITH

Epilogue to *She Stoops to Conquer*

Well, having stoop'd to conquer with success,
And gain'd a husband without aid from dress,
Still, as a Barmaid, I could wish it too,
As I have conquer'd him, to conquer you:
And let me say, for all your resolution,
That pretty Barmaids have done execution.
Our life is all a play, compos'd to please,
'We have our exits and our entrances.'
The First Act shows the simple country maid,
Harmless and young, of ev'ry thing afraid;
Blushes when hir'd and, with unmeaning action,
'I hope as how to give you satisfaction.'
Her Second Act displays a livelier scene –
Th' unblushing Barmaid of a country inn,

41

Who whisks about the house, at market caters,
Talks loud, coquets the guests, and scolds the waiters.
Next the scene shifts to town, and there she soars,
The chop-house toast of ogling connoisseurs.
On 'Squires and Cits she there displays her arts,
And on the gridiron broils her lovers' hearts:
And as she smiles, her triumphs to complete,
Even Common-Councilmen forget to eat.
The Fourth Act shows her wedded to the 'Squire,
And Madam now begins to hold it higher;
Pretends to taste, at Operas cries *caro*,
And quits her *Nancy Dawson*, for *Che faro*,
Doats upon dancing, and in all her pride,
Swims round the room, the Heinel of Cheapside;
Ogles and leers with artificial skill,
'Till having lost in age the power to kill,
She sits all night at cards, and ogles at spadille.
Such, through our lives, the eventful history –
The Fifth and Last Act still remains for me.
The Barmaid now for your protection prays,
Turns Female Barrister, and pleads for Bayes.

Epilogue to *The Sister: A Comedy*

What! five long acts – and all to make us wiser!
Our authoress sure has wanted an adviser.
Had she consulted *me*, she should have made
Her moral play a speaking masquerade,
Warm'd up each bustling scene, and in her rage
Have emptied all the Green-room on the stage.
My life on't, this had kept her play from sinking,
Have pleas'd our eyes, and sav'd the pain of thinking.
Well, since she thus has shewn her want of skill,
What if I give a masquerade? I will.
But how! ay, there's the rub! (*pausing*) I've got my cue:
The world's a masquerade! the masquers, you, you, you.

Lud! what a groupe the motley scene discloses!
False wits, false wives, false virgins, and false spouses:
Statesmen with bridles on; and, close beside 'em,
Patriots, in part colour'd suits, that ride 'em.
There Hebes, turn'd of fifty, try once more,
To raise a flame in Cupids of threescore.
These, in their turn, with appetites as keen,
Deserting fifty, fasten on fifteen.
Miss, not yet full fifteen, with fire uncommon,
Flings down her sampler, and takes up the woman:
The little urchin smiles, and spreads her lure,
And tries to kill ere she's got power to cure.
Thus 'tis with all – Their chief and constant care

43

Is to seem every thing – but what they are.
Yon broad, bold, angry, spark, I fix my eye on,
Who seems t' have robb'ed his visor from the lion,
Who frowns, and talks, and swears, with round parade,
Looking as who should say, *Damme! who's afraid!*
Strip but his vizor off, and sure I am,
You'll find his lionship a very lamb.
Yon politician, famous in debate,
Perhaps to vulgar eyes bestrides the state;
Yet, when he deigns his real shape t' assume,
He turns old woman, and bestrides a broom.
Yon patriot too, who presses on your sight,
And seems to every gazer all in white;
If with a bribe his candour you attack,
He bows, turns round, and whip – the man's a black!
If I proceed, our bard will be undone!
Well then, a truce, since she requests it too;
Do you spare her, and I'll for once spare you.

Translations from *An History of the Earth, and Animated Nature*

I

Of all the fish that graze beneath the flood,
He only ruminates his former food.

2

Chaste are their instincts, faithful is their fire,
No foreign beauty tempts to false desire:
The snow-white vesture, and the glittering crown,
The simple plumage, or the glossy down,
Prompt not their love. The patriot bird pursues
His well acquainted tints, and kindred hues.
Hence through their tribes no mix'd polluted flame,
No monster breed to mark the groves with shame:
But the chaste blackbird, to its partner true,
Thinks black alone is beauty's favourite hue:
The nightingale, with mutual passion blest,
Sings to its mate, and nightly charms the nest:
While the dark owl, to court his partner flies,
And owns his offspring in their yellow eyes.

The Haunch Of Venison

Thanks, my Lord, for your venison, for finer or fatter
Never rang'd in a forest, or smok'd in a platter;
The haunch was a picture for painters to study,
The fat was so white, and the lean was so ruddy.
Though my stomach was sharp, I could scarce help
    regretting
To spoil such a delicate picture by eating;
I had thoughts, in my chambers, to place it in view,
To be shown to my friends as a piece of *virtù*;
As in some Irish houses, where things are so so,
One gammon of bacon hangs up for a show:
But for eating a rasher of what they take pride in,
They'd as soon think of eating the pan it is fried in.
But hold – let me pause – Don't I hear you pronounce
This tale of the bacon a damnable bounce?
Well, suppose it a bounce – sure a poet may try,
By a bounce now and then, to get courage to fly.

But, my Lord, it's no bounce: I protest in my turn,
It's a truth – and your Lordship may ask Mr Byrne.
To go on with my tale – as I gaz'd on the haunch,
I thought of a friend that was trusty and staunch;
So I cut it, and sent it to Reynolds undress'd.
To paint it, or eat it, just as he lik'd best.
Of the neck and the breast I had next to dispose;

46

'Twas a neck and a breast – that might rival M–r–'s:
But in parting with these I was puzzled again,
With the how, and the who, and the where, and the when.
There's H–d, and C–y, and H–rth, and H–ff,
I think they love venison – I know they love beef;
There's my countryman H–gg–ns – Oh! let him alone,
For making a blunder, or picking a bone.
But hang it – to poets who seldom can eat,
Your very good mutton's a very good treat;
Such dainties to them, their health it might hurt,
It's like sending them ruffles, when wanting a shirt.
While thus I debated, in reverie centred,
An acquaintance, a friend as he call'd himself, enter'd;
An under-bred, fine-spoken fellow was he,
And he smil'd as he look'd at the venison and me.
'What have we got here? – Why, this is good eating!
Your own, I suppose – or is it in waiting?'
'Why, whose should it be?' cried I with a flounce,
'I get these things often;' – but that was a bounce;
'Some lords, my acquaintance, that settle the nation,
Are pleas'd to be kind – but I hate ostentation.'

'If that be the case, then,' cried he, very gay,
'I'm glad I have taken this house in my way.
Tomorrow you take a poor dinner with me;
No words – I insist on't – precisely at three;
We'll have Johnson, and Burke; all the wits will be there;
My acquaintance is slight, or I'd ask my Lord Clare.
And now that I think on't, as I am a sinner!

We wanted this venison to make out the dinner.
What say you – a pasty? it shall, and it must,
And my wife, little Kitty, is famous for crust.
Here, porter! – this venison with me to Mile-end;
No stirring – I beg – my dear friend – my dear friend!'
Thus snatching his hat, he brush'd off like the wind,
And the porter and eatables follow'd behind.

Left alone to reflect, having emptied my shelf,
'And nobody with me at sea but myself';
Though I could not help thinking my gentleman hasty,
Yet Johnson, and Burke, and a good venison pasty,
Were things that I never dislik'd in my life,
Though clogg'd with a coxcomb, and Kitty his wife.
So next day, in due splendour to make my approach,
I drove to his door in my own own hackney coach.

When come to the place where we all were to dine,
(A chair-lumber'd closet just twelve feet by nine:)
My friend bade me welcome, but struck me quite dumb,
With tidings that Johnson and Burke would not come;
'For I knew it,' he cried, 'both eternally fail,
The one with his speeches, and t'other with Thrale;
But no matter, I'll warrant we'll make up the party
With two full as clever, and ten minutes as hearty.
The one is a Scotchman, the other a Jew,
They['re] both of them merry and authors like you;
The one writes the *Snarler*, the other the *Scourge*;
Some think he writes *Cinna* – he owns to *Panurge*.'

While thus he describ'd them by trade, and by name,
They enter'd, and dinner was serv'd as they came.

At the top a fried liver and bacon were seen,
At the bottom was tripe in a swinging tureen;
At the sides there was spinach and pudding made hot
In the middle a place where the pasty – was not.
Now, my Lord, as for tripe, it's my utter aversion,
And your bacon I hate like a Turk or a Persian;
So there I sat stuck, like a horse in a pound,
While the bacon and liver went merrily round.
But what vex'd me most was that d–'d Scottish rogue
With his long-winded speeches, his smiles and his brogue;
And, 'Madam,' quoth he, 'may this bit be my poison,
A prettier dinner I never set eyes on;
Pray a slice of your liver, though may I be curs'd,
But I've eat of your tripe till I'm ready to burst.'
'The tripe,' quoth the Jew, with his chocolate cheek,
'I could dine on this tripe seven days in the week:
I like these here dinners so pretty and small;
But your friend there, the Doctor, eats nothing at all.'
'O – Oh!' quoth my friend, 'he'll come on in a trice,
He's keeping a corner for something that's nice:
There's a pasty' – 'A pasty!' repeated the Jew,
'I don't care if I keep a corner for't too.'
'What the de'il, mon, a pasty!' re-echoed the Scot,
'Though splitting, I'll still keep a corner for thot.'
'We'll all keep a corner,' the lady cried out;

49

'We'll all keep a corner,' was echoed about.
While thus we resolv'd, and the pasty delay'd,
With looks that quite petrified, enter'd the maid;
A visage so sad, and so pale with affright,
Wak'd Priam in drawing his curtains by night.
But we quickly found out, for who could mistake her?
That she came with some terrible news from the baker:
And so it fell out, for that negligent sloven
Had shut out the pasty on shutting his oven
Sad Philomel thus – but let similes drop –
And now that I think on't, the story may stop.
To be plain, my good Lord, it's but labour misplac'd
To send such good verses to one of your taste;
You've got an old something – a kind of discerning –
A relish – a taste – sicken'd over by learning;
At least, it's your temper, as very well known,
That you think very slightly of all that's your own:
So, perhaps, in your habits of thinking amiss,
You may make a mistake, and think slightly of this.

The Clown's Reply

John Trott was desired by two witty peers
To tell them the reason why asses had ears?
'An't please you,' quoth John, 'I'm not given to letters.
Nor dare I pretend to know more than my betters;
Howe'er, from this time I shall ne'er see your graces,
As I hope to be saved! without thinking on asses.'

Epitaph on Edward Purdon

Here lies poor Ned Purdon, from misery freed,
   Who long was a bookseller's hack;
He led such a damnable life in this world, –
   I don't think he'll wish to come back.

Epilogue

Intended to have been spoken for She Stoops to Conquer

There is a place, so Ariosto sings,
A treasury for lost and missing things:
Lost human wits have places there assign'd them,
And they, who lose their senses, there may find them.
But where's this place, this storehouse of the age?
The Moon, says he: but *I* affirm the Stage:

At least in many things, I think, I see
His lunar, and our mimic world agree.
Both shine at night, for, but at Foote's alone,
We scarce exhibit till the sun goes down.
Both prone to change, no settled limits fix.
And sure the folks of both are lunatics.
But in this parallel my best pretence is,
That mortals visit both to find their senses.
To this strange spot, Rakes, Macaronies, Cits,
Come thronging to collect their scatter'd wits.
The gay coquette, who ogles all the day,
Comes here at night, and goes a prude away.
Hither the affected city dame advancing,
Who sighs for operas, and dotes on dancing,
Taught by our art her ridicule to pause on,
Quits the *Ballet*, and calls for *Nancy Dawson*.
The Gamester too, whose wit 's all high or low,
Oft risks his fortune on one desperate throw,
Comes here to saunter, having made his bets,
Finds his lost senses out, and pay his debts.
The Mohawk too – with angry phrases stored,
As 'D—, Sir,' and 'Sir, I wear a sword';
Here lesson'd for a while, and hence retreating,
Goes out, affronts his man, and takes a beating.
Here come the sons of scandal and of news,
But find no sense – for they had none to lose.
Of all the tribe here wanting an adviser
Our Author's the least likely to grow wiser;

Has he not seen how you your favour place,
On sentimental Queens and Lords in lace?
Without a star, a coronet or garter,
How can the piece expect or hope for quarter?
No high-life scenes, no sentiment: – the creature
Still stoops among the low to copy nature.
Yes, he's far gone: – and yet some pity fix,
The English laws forbid to punish lunatics.

Letter to Mrs Bunbury

First let me suppose what may shortly be true
The company set, and the word to be Loo.
All smirking, and pleasant, and big with adventure
And ogling the stake which is fixd in the center.
Round and round go the cards while I inwardly damn
At never once finding a visit from Pam.
I lay down my stake, apparently cool,
While the harpies about me all pocket the pool.
I fret in my gizzard, yet cautious and sly
I wish all my friends may be bolder than I.
Yet still they sit snugg, not a creature will aim
By losing their money to venture at fame.
Tis in vain that at niggardly caution I scold
Tis in vain that I flatter the brave and the bold
All play in their own way, and think me an ass.
What does Mrs Bunbury? I sir? I pass.

Pray what does Miss Horneck? Take courage. Come do.
Who I! Let me see sir. Why I must pass too.
Mr Bunbury frets, and I fret like the devil
To see them so cowardly lucky and civil.
Yet still I set snugg and continue to sigh on
Till made by my losses as bold as a lion
I venture at all, while my avarice regards
The whole pool as my own. Come give me five cards.
Well done cry the ladies. Ah Doctor that's good.
The pool's very rich. Ah. The Doctor is lood.
Thus foild in my courage, on all sides perplext,
I ask for advice from the lady that's next
Pray mam be so good as to give your advice
Dont you think the best way is to venture fort twice.
I advise cries the lady to try it I own.
Ah! The Doctor is lood. Come Doctor, put down.
Thus playing and playing I still grow more eager
And so bold and so bold, Im at last a bold beggar.
Now ladies I ask if law matters youre skilld in
Whether crimes such as yours should not come before
     Fielding
For giving advice that is not worth a straw
May well be call'd picking of pockets in law
And picking of pockets with which I now charge ye
is by Quinto Elizabeth death without Clergy.
What justice when both to the Old Baily brought
By the gods Ill enjoy it, tho' 'tis but in thought.

Both are placed at the bar with all proper decorum

With bunches of Fennel and nosegays before em.
Both cover their faces with mobbs and all that
But the judge bids them angrily take of their hat.
When uncovered a buzz of enquiry runs round
Pray what are their crimes? Theyv'e been pilfering found.
But pray who have they pilfered? A Doctor I hear.
When yon solemn fac'd odd looking man that stands near.
The same. What a pitty. How does it surprize one
Two handsomer culprits I never set eyes on.
Then their friends all come round me with cringing and
    leering
To melt me to pitty, and soften my swearing.
First Sir Charles advances, with phrases well strung
Consider Dear Doctor the girls are but young.
The younger the Worse I return him again.
Its shews that their habits are all dy'd in grain.
But then theyre so handsome, one's bosom it grieves.
What signifies handsome, when people are thieves.
But where is your justice; their cases are hard.
What signifies justice; I want the reward.
But consider their case. It may yet be your own
And see how they kneel; is your heart made of stone?
This moves, so at last I agree to relent
For ten pounds in hand, and ten pound to be spent
The judge takes the hint, having seen what we drive at
And lets them both off with correction in private.

A Note on Oliver Goldsmith

Oliver Goldsmith (1730–74), the English dramatist, poet, and essayist, was born probably at Pallasmore, County Longford, the son of an Anglo-Irish clergyman. His family later lived at Lissoy, and he was educated at various schools at Elgin, Athlone, and Edgeworthstown. At the age of eight he had a severe attack of smallpox which left him disfigured. In 1744 Goldsmith went as a sizar to Trinity College, Dublin, but in 1747, having been humiliated by one of the tutors, he ran away. Induced to return, he graduated BA in 1749.

In 1752 he went to Edinburgh to study medicine, and in 1753 proceeded to Leyden, ostensibly to continue his studies. After a year there he started on a walking tour through France, Germany, Switzerland, and Italy. He left Leyden penniless, and is supposed to have earned a living by disputing at universities and playing the flute. However, he was gaining experience and knowledge which he afterwards used in his writings. At one of the universities he visited, Goldsmith is said to have secured a medical degree.

He reached London in 1756, almost penniless, and

appears to have worked as an apothecary's journeyman, a doctor, and an usher in a school at Peckham, London. In 1757 he was writing for the *Monthly Review* and the next year applied unsuccessfully for a medical appointment in India. In 1759 his first important literary venture, *An Enquiry into the Present State of Polite Learning in Europe*, was published anonymously; it attracted some attention and brought other work. At the same time he became known to Bishop Percy, then collecting his *Reliques of Ancient Poetry*. He also wrote *The Bee*, a collection of essays, and was employed on various periodicals. In 1761 Goldsmith became friendly with Dr Johnson, and other members of his circle, and became a founder member of 'The Club'. His *Chinese Letters*, afterwards republished as *The Citizen of the World*, first appeared in 1760. *The Traveller: or a Prospect of Society*, the first of his longer poems, was issued in 1764, and was followed in 1766 by his novel *The Vicar of Wakefield: A Tale*. In 1768 his drama, *The Good Natur'd Man: A Comedy*, had considerable success.

During the next few yeras, Goldsmith was busily occupied with works for publishers, including *The History of Rome*, 1769, and lives of Parnell, the poet, and Lord Bolingbroke, 1770; in the same year *The Deserted Village* appeared. The poem combines nostalgia for a lost past (Auburn in the poem is based on Lissoy) with a keen economic awareness. In 1773 he produced his other drama, the famous *She Stoops to Conquer, or The Mistakes of a*

Night. A Comedy, with great success. His last works were *Retaliation: A Poem, The History of Greece,* and *An History of the Earth, and Animated Nature,* all published in 1774. In that year, worn out with overwork and anxiety, he caught fever and died.

Other titles in this series

Andrew Marvell   *To His Coy Mistress*

John Milton   *Paradise Lost*

Wilfred Owen   *The Pity of War*

Palgrave   *Golden Treasury of Love Poems*

Edgar Allan Poe   *The Raven*

Alexander Pope   *The Rape of the Lock*

Christina Rossetti   *Goblin Market*

Sir Walter Scott   *Lochinvar*

William Shakespeare   *Love Sonnets*

Percy Bysshe Shelley   *To a Skylark*

Edmund Spenser   *The Fairy Queen*

Alfred, Lord Tennyson   *The Lady of Shalott*

Dylan Thomas   *Fern Hill*

Edward Thomas   *There Was a Time*

R. S. Thomas   *Love Poems*

Francis Thompson   *The Hound of Heaven*

Walt Whitman   *I Sing the Body Electric*

William Wordsworth   *Intimations of Immortality*

W. B. Yeats   *Sailing to Byzantium*